GAUGUIN

PAVILION
MICHAEL JOSEPH

D0521471

First published in Great Britain in 1989 by
Pavilion Books Limited
196 Shaftesbury Avenue, London WC2H 8JL
in association with Michael Joseph Limited
27 Wrights Lane, Kensington, London W8 5TZ

Text Copyright © Pavilion Books 1989
Illustrations – Copyright and sources as indicated
on the back of each card

Designed by Bridgewater Design Limited

ISBN: 1-85145-448-9

Printed and bound in Singapore by Imago Publishing Limited

10   9   8   7   6   5   4   3   2   1

FOREWORD

Such has been the influence of Paul Gauguin (1848-1903) since his death that the pattern of his life seems all the more perverse. In his twenties Gauguin was a prosperous Parisian stockbroker and family man who admired and collected the Impressionists and painted as a hobby, whereas the last two decades of his life were spent in ever deeper poverty and isolation as he moved further and further away from his social and artistic roots.

After meeting Pissarro in 1875 he began to exhibit with the Impressionists, and within ten years he had left both job and family to concentrate on painting. The years 1886-1890, spent mostly in Brittany, saw Gauguin turning away from Impressionism and developing a highly individual style characterized by large areas of bold colours and strong contrasts. In 1891, drawn to the simple, intuitive existence of primitive peoples, he left for the South Seas, where his most powerful and haunting work was done and where, after an unhappy two-year return to France, he died in 1903.

Gauguin's exoticism and rejection of western civilization led in the short term to the cult of primitivism; it is, however, his use of colour and his concern that art should reflect man's inner life rather than naturalistic detail that make Gauguin one of the fathers of modern painting.

PAUL GAUGUIN (1843-1903)
Autoportrait (Self Portrait)
MUSÉE D'ORSAY, PARIS

PUBLISHED BY PAVILION BOOKS LIMITED

PAUL GAUGUIN (1843-1903)
La Seine au Pont d'Iena, Temps de Neige
(The Seine with Iena Bridge in the Snow)
MUSÉE D'ORSAY, PARIS

PUBLISHED BY PAVILION BOOKS LIMITED

PAUL GAUGUIN (1843-1903)
Nature Morte aux Oranges (Still Life with Oranges)
MUSÉE DES BEAUX-ARTS, RENNES / BRIDGEMAN ART LIBRARY, LONDON

PUBLISHED BY PAVILION BOOKS LIMITED

PAUL GAUGUIN (1843-1903)
La Neige, Rue Carcel (The Snow, Rue Carcel)
KAIER COLLECTION, COPENHAGEN / BRIDGEMAN ART LIBRARY,
LONDON

PUBLISHED BY PAVILION BOOKS LIMITED

PAUL GAUGUIN (1843-1903)
La Plage à Dieppe (The Beach at Dieppe)
PRIVATE COLLECTION / BRIDGEMAN ART LIBRARY, LONDON

PUBLISHED BY PAVILION BOOKS LIMITED

P A U L   G A U G U I N (1843-1903)
Les Quatre Bretonnes (The Four Bretons)
STAATLICHE ANTIKENSAMMLUNG, MUNICH/
BRIDGEMAN ART LIBRARY, LONDON

P U B L I S H E D   B Y   P A V I L I O N   B O O K S   L I M I T E D

PAUL GAUGUIN (1843-1903)
La Bergère Bretonne (Breton Shepherdess)
LAING ART GALLERY, NEWCASTLE-UPON-TYNE/
BRIDGEMAN ART LIBRARY, LONDON

PUBLISHED BY PAVILION BOOKS LIMITED

PAUL GAUGUIN (1843-1903)
Les Vaches à L'Abreuvoir (Cows at the Watering Place)
GALLERIA D'ARTE MODERNA, MILAN/
BRIDGEMAN ART LIBRARY, LONDON

PUBLISHED BY PAVILION BOOKS LIMITED

PAUL GAUGUIN (1843-1903)
La Famille du Peintre au Jardin (The Family of the Painter in the Garden)
NY CARLSBERG GLYPTOTEK, COPENHAGEN /
BRIDGEMAN ART LIBRARY, LONDON

PUBLISHED BY PAVILION BOOKS LIMITED

PAUL GAUGUIN (1843-1903)
Paysage de Bretagne (Landscape in Brittany)
MUSÉE D'ORSAY, PARIS

PUBLISHED BY PAVILION BOOKS LIMITED

PAUL GAUGUIN (1843-1903)
Les Alyscamps
MUSÉE D'ORSAY, PARIS

PUBLISHED BY PAVILION BOOKS LIMITED

PAUL GAUGUIN (1843-1903)
La Famille Schuffenecker (The Schuffenecker Family)
MUSÉE D'ORSAY, PARIS

PUBLISHED BY PAVILION BOOKS LIMITED

PAUL GAUGUIN (1843-1903)
Les Meules Jaunes ou la Moisson Blonde
(Yellow Haystacks or Golden Harvest)
MUSÉE D'ORSAY, PARIS

PUBLISHED BY PAVILION BOOKS LIMITED

PAUL GAUGUIN (1843-1903)
La Belle Angèle (The Beautiful Angela)
MUSÉE D'ORSAY, PARIS

PUBLISHED BY PAVILION BOOKS LIMITED

PAUL GAUGUIN (1843-1903)
La Plage à Pouldu (The Beach at Pouldu)
PRIVATE COLLECTION / BRIDGEMAN ART LIBRARY

PUBLISHED BY PAVILION BOOKS LIMITED

P U B L I S H E D B Y P A V I L I O N B O O K S L I M I T E D

PAUL GAUGUIN (1843-1903)
Ramasseuses de Varech (The Seaweed Harvesters)
FOLKWANG MUSEUM, ESSEN / BRIDGEMAN ART LIBRARY, LONDON

PUBLISHED BY PAVILION BOOKS LIMITED

PAUL GAUGUIN (1843-1903)
Paysannes bretonnes (Breton Peasants)
MUSÉE D'ORSAY, PARIS

PUBLISHED BY PAVILION BOOKS LIMITED

PAUL GAUGUIN (1843-1903)
Café de Nuit à Arles (Night Café at Arles)
MUSEUM OF WESTERN ART, MOSCOW/
BRIDGEMAN ART LIBRARY, LONDON

PUBLISHED BY PAVILION BOOKS LIMITED

PAUL GAUGUIN (1843-1903)
Le Repas (The Meal)
MUSÉE D'ORSAY, PARIS

PUBLISHED BY PAVILION BOOKS LIMITED

PAUL GAUGUIN (1843-1903)
Femmes de Tahiti Sur la Plage (Tahitian Women on the Beach)
MUSÉE D'ORSAY, PARIS

PUBLISHED BY PAVILION BOOKS LIMITED

PAUL GAUGUIN (1843-1903)
Le Cheval Blanc (The White Horse)
MUSÉE D'ORSAY, PARIS

PUBLISHED BY PAVILION BOOKS LIMITED

PAUL GAUGUIN (1843-1903)
Ea Haero Ia Oe Go!
HERMITAGE, LENINGRAD / BRIDGEMAN ART LIBRARY, LONDON

PUBLISHED BY PAVILION BOOKS LIMITED

PAUL GAUGUIN (1843-1903)
Pastorales Tahitiennes
THE HERMITAGE, LENINGRAD / BRIDGEMAN ART LIBRARY, LONDON

PUBLISHED BY PAVILION BOOKS LIMITED

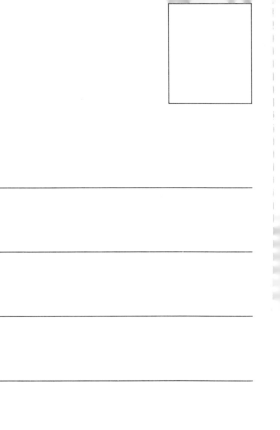

PAUL GAUGUIN (1843-1903)
Nave Nave Mahana
MUSÉE DES BEAUX-ARTS, PARIS / BRIDGEMAN ART LIBRARY, LONDON

PUBLISHED BY PAVILION BOOKS LIMITED

PAUL GAUGUIN (1843-1903)
Arearea
MUSÉE D'ORSAY, PARIS

PUBLISHED BY PAVILION BOOKS LIMITED

PAUL GAUGUIN (1843-1903)
La Maison des Chants (The House of Song)

PUBLISHED BY PAVILION BOOKS LIMITED

PAUL GAUGUIN (1843-1903)
A detail from *Faa Iheihe*
THE TATE GALLERY, LONDON

PUBLISHED BY PAVILION BOOKS LIMITED

PAUL GAUGUIN (1843-1903)
Juene Fille à L'Eventail (Girl with Fan)
MUSEUM FOLKWANG, ESSEN / BRIDGEMAN ART LIBRARY, LONDON

PUBLISHED BY PAVILION BOOKS LIMITED

PAUL GAUGUIN (1843-1903)
Album Ancien Culte Mahori
MUSÉE D'ORSAY, PARIS

PUBLISHED BY PAVILION BOOKS LIMITED